Greatest Giggles Ever

Matt Rissinger and Philip Yates

Illustrated by Jeff Sinclair

Sterling Publishing Co., Inc.
New York

To my giggly girls–Rebecca, Emily, and
Abigail–Love, MR

To John and Susan, and Benta, Ian, and
Christian–Love, PY

10　9　8　7　6　5　4　3　2　1

Library of Congress Cataloging-in-Publication Data Available

Published by Sterling Publishing Company, Inc.
387 Park Avenue South, New York, N.Y. 10016
© 2002 by Matt Rissinger and Philip Yates
Distributed in Canada by Sterling Publishing
c/o Canadian Manda Group, One Atlantic Avenue, Suite 105
Toronto, Ontario, Canada M6K 3E7
Distributed in Great Britain and Europe by Chris Lloyd
at Orca Book Services, Stanley House, Fleets Lane,
Poole BH15 3AJ, England
Distributed in Australia by Capricorn Link (Australia) Pty. Ltd.
P.O. Box 704, Windsor, NSW 2756 Australia

Sterling ISBN 0-8069-9025-2

Contents

1. Zoo-Purr Dooper

Where do cows, pigs, sheep, ducks, and horses go to get their prescriptions filled?

Old MacDonald's Farm-Acy.

What do you call a deer that yells out road instructions?

A buck seat driver.

What's the hardest thing for elephants who play football?

Squeezing into the huddle.

Where would you find a fire-fighting dinosaur?
Jurassic Spark.

What would you get if you crossed a dinosaur with a chicken?
Tyrannosaurus Pecks.

DILL: What would you get if you crossed a dinosaur and an ant?

WILL: I don't know, but I bet it's no fun at a picnic.

How is a kid who loves dinosaurs like a paleontologist?
They both dig dinosaurs.

What dinosaur loved to barbecue?
Steak-a-saurus.

What dinosaur loved to be tickled with a feather?
Giggle-o-saurus.

Where did T. Rex park his convertible?
In a Jurassic Parking lot.

FLIP: What do you get when ten ducks driving east
   on the freeway run into ten ducks driving west?
FLOP: A twenty-duck quack-up. .

Who's a goose's favorite movie star?
Tom Honks.

How do parameciums call home?
On single-cell phones.

How did the skunk call home?
He used his smell phone.

How does Miss Muffett call home?
On her curd-less phone.

Why couldn't the talkative little rabbit call home?
He used up all his cell phone's hare time.

What would you get if you crossed a dragon and the
best man at a wedding?
A guy who really knows how to toast the bride and groom.

Why don't people like to take checks from kangaroos?
Because their checks might bounce.

What kind of pig would you find on the Evening News?
An oinkerman.

What would you get if you crossed Miss Piggy with a beauty queen?
Mess America.

What would you get if you crossed a small hog and a Frenchman?
A little pig that goes "Oui, oui, oui" all the way home.

What would you get if you crossed a parrot with a pig?
A squawky bird that hogs the conversation.

SNIP: What is Porky Pig's favorite winter sport?
SNAP: Ice hoggy.

What's a pig's favorite kind of comedy?
Slopstick.

Where does Bullwinkle keep his old pictures and collectables?
In a moose-eum.

How do mice celebrate when they move into a new home?
With a mouse-warming party!

What do frogs drink for breakfast?
Hot croako with marshmallows.

What would you get if you crossed a frog with a cloud?
Kermit the Fog!

What bear likes to swim and has big sharp teeth?
A bear-a-cuda!

What bears like to swim but can't fit into bathing suits?
Bare-a-cudas!

What animal always takes a bath with its shoes on?
A horse!

Why did the crab cross the road?
To get to the other tide!

What do you call a fish with no eyes?
Fsh!

What romantic song do fish sing?
"Salmon-chanted evening!"

What did the shrimp do with the big diamond ring?
He prawned it!

What do you get from a bad-tempered shark?
As far away as possible!

SLIM: Do sharks tell lies?
JIM: No, they're usually very toothful.

Where did the shellfish kiss Santa Claus?
Under the mussel toe.

GERT: What does a mermaid take to stay healthy?
BERT: Vitamin sea.

What would you get if you crossed a huge sea creature and a chicken?
A hump-buck-buck whale.

Why was the young whale sent to the principal?
For spouting off at the teacher.

Why did the pelican refuse to pay for his meal?
His bill was too big.

Where do penguins keep their money?
In snow banks.

How does an octopus go to war?
Well armed!

Who held the octopus for ransom?
Squidnappers!

What's gray, wrinkly, and quivers every twenty seconds?
An elephant with hiccups!

Why are elephants gray?
So you can tell them from flamingos!

How is an elephant like a hippopotamus?
Neither can play basketball!

WILLIE: How am I going to write an essay on an
elephant?
TILLIE: First, you're going to need a big ladder.

TED: How do you know when there's an elephant in
your peanut butter?
ZED: Read the list of ingredients.

12

What do you call ten monkeys marooned on a island?
Chimp-wrecked.

What piece of music do monkeys play in an orchestra?
A chimp-phony.

What nutty chicken tells you the time?
A cuckoo cluck!

What would you get if you crossed a chicken and a lazy worker?
A bird that lays down on the job.

What do you call a half dozen chickens crossing the street?
A six peck!

What is a parrot's favorite game?
Hide 'n' Speak!

What school do you send a parrot to?
Polly-technical!

Why don't ducks enjoy the desert?
They're afraid of quacksand.

What is a duck's favorite soda?
Quack-a-Cola.

CHAD: Why did the cat eat two birds?
BRAD: The second bird was an after dinner tweet.

Did you hear about the cats that moved next door to the mice?
They wanted to have the neighbors over for dinner.

What kind of healthy cereal do mice eat?
Squeaker Oats.

What do mice do on Halloween?
They go to mousequerade parties.

What kind of jokes do mice tell?
Squeaky clean ones.

What kind of jokes do camels tell?
Hump-dingers.

2. Shriek, Rattle & Roar

What classic TV comedy deals with ghosts stranded on an island?

Ghoul-igan's Island.

What do little ghosts wear when it rains?

Boo-ts and ghoul-oshes!

Why was the ghost rushed to the hospital?

To have its ghoul bladder removed.

What would you get if you crossed a ghost and a groundhog?

A phantom who's afraid of its own shadow.

15

What would you get if you crossed Lizzie Borden with a groundhog?

Six more whacks of winter.

How do you get rid of Lizzie Borden's ghost?

Call an Ax-orcist.

Who is a ghost's favorite rock star?

Boos Springsteen.

What would you get if you crossed a razor with a ghost?

Shaving scream.

What's a ghost's favorite ride at Disneyland?

The Moan-o-Rail.

What has two heads and eats luxury hotel rooms?

A monster with a suite tooth.

HOMER: Did you hear about the monster with five legs?

GOMER: No, but I bet his pants fit him like a glove.

Why don't really hungry monsters like to eat mummies?

It takes too long to get the wrappers off.

GHASTLY BEST SELLERS

Swimming with Sharks	by Mya Watt Beegteef
My Mother Was a Werewolf	by Sheila Tack Hugh
My Doctor Was a Vampire	by E. Drew Bludd
I Was Possessed	by Eve L. Spirit
The Hungry Monster	by Aida Lotte

Why did the monster give up boxing?
He didn't want to spoil his good looks.

What kind of television set would you find in a monster's house?
A big-scream TV.

What's a ghoul's favorite soup?
Scream of tomb-ato.

What's a weirdo's favorite soda?
Kook-a-Cola.

What London slasher worked in an ice cream shoppe?
Jack the Ripple.

FUZZY: Do vampires dance?
WUZZY: Yes, they do the fang-dango.

DILLY: Do vampires act in movies?
SILLY: Yes, they get bit parts.

What's a vampire's favorite ice cream?
  Vein-illa.

What would you get if you crossed an author and a vampire?
  A book you can really sink your teeth into.

What would you get if you crossed a vampire with a duck?
  Count Quackula.

What would you get if you crossed a vampire with a crime fighter?
  Drac Tracy.

Did you hear about the vampire who was a failure?
  He fainted at the sight of blood.

What would you get if you crossed a Viking and a vampire?
  A pretty bad Norse-bleed.

What's a vampire's favorite car?

A Luxury Necks-us Sedan.

Why did the vampire want a raise?

He was tired of making necks to nothing.

What was Dracula's favorite hobby?

Casket-weaving.

DILL: Was Dracula ever married?

WILL: No, he's always been a bat-chelor.

Why didn't the Abominable Snowman get married?

He got cold feet.

What's worse than a three-headed dragon?
A three-headed dragon with bad breath.

What is the Invisible Man's favorite music channel?
Empty-V.

What was the Invisible Man raised on?
Evaporated milk.

Why did the Invisible Man's son flunk third grade?
His teacher kept marking him absent.

What do you do with a zombie race car driver?
Ex-zoom him.

Why did the zombies go down with the *Titanic*?
They refused to get into a lifeboat.

NIT: What's hairy and goes "Hic-hic-howl"?
WIT: A werewolf with hiccups.

What day is unlucky for a werewolf?
Friday the Fur-teenth.

MONSTER: I think I've changed my mind.
DR. FRANKENSTEIN: Good, does the new one work any
   better?

What is evil and ugly on the inside and green on the outside?

A wicked witch disguised as a cucumber!

What has six legs and flies?

A witch giving her cat a ride!

What is gruesome, flies, and goes "Cough-cough"?

A witch in a dust storm!

What is evil and ugly and bounces up and down?

A witch on a trampoline!

Why did the little witch come to school dressed as a spoon?

She wanted to stir things up.

Why did the witch fly through the car wash?
She wanted a clean sweep!

What would you get if you crossed a canary and a wizard?
Cheep tricks.

SHAGGY WIZARD STORY

An evil wizard, in order to take over the world, made several replicas of himself. When the townsfolk found out, they sent some gnomes to do battle with the wizard. Armed with spears and rocks, the gnomes managed to drive the duplicate wizards out of the country. As he sped off on his magic broom, the wizard shouted: "Sticks and stones may break my clones, but gnomes will never hurt me."

What bunny goes to sorcerer school?
Hare E. Potter.

Why did Harry Potter attach a camcorder to his Nimbus 2000?
He wanted a broom with a view.

What sci-fi movie features lots of fancy French desserts?
Planet of the Crepes.

What *Star Wars* character is always taking the long route?
R2 Detour.

What would you get if you crossed a spaceship with Tex-Mex?
Flying salsa.

Why did young Luke Skywalker always sleep with the night-light on?
He was afraid of the Darth.

What's the difference between Luke Skywalker and a cheap late night flight?
One's a Jedi, the other's a redeye.

What *Star Wars* movie features a classical composer?
The Empire Strikes Bach.

What beetle comes from outer space?
Bug Rogers.

DILL: Why did Captain Kirk enter the ladies' room?
WILL: He wanted to go where no man had gone before!

What illness did everyone on the *Enterprise* catch?
Chicken Spocks!

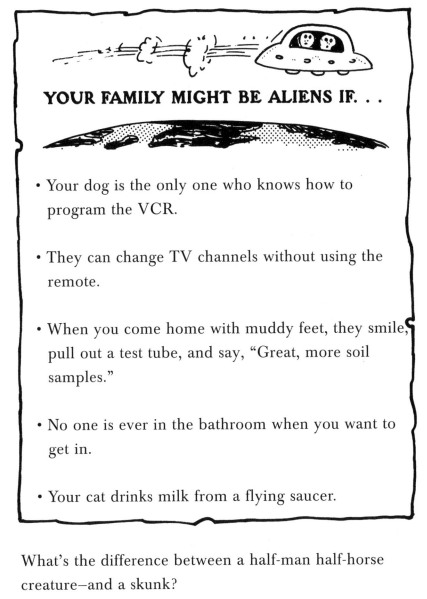

YOUR FAMILY MIGHT BE ALIENS IF. . .

- Your dog is the only one who knows how to program the VCR.

- They can change TV channels without using the remote.

- When you come home with muddy feet, they smile, pull out a test tube, and say, "Great, more soil samples."

- No one is ever in the bathroom when you want to get in.

- Your cat drinks milk from a flying saucer.

What's the difference between a half-man half-horse creature—and a skunk?

One is a centaur and the other is a scent-er.

What do dweebs do on Halloween?

They carve faces on apples and bob for pumpkins!

3. Fractured Funnies

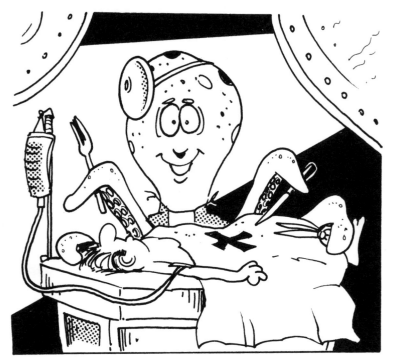

What do you call a surgeon with eight arms?
A doc-topus.

PATIENT: Doctor, doctor, I have a burning stomach
pain and a blazing fever.
DOCTOR: You don't need a doctor, you need a fireman.

PATIENT: Doctor, doctor, I had a dream I ate a five-
pound marshmallow and when I woke up, my pillow
was missing.
DOCTOR: I find that hard to swallow.

What would you get if you crossed a massage therapist and a bully?

Someone who really rubs you the wrong way.

PATIENT: Doctor, I keep losing my temper.
DOCTOR: Would you care to tell me about it?
PATIENT: I just did, you stupid idiot!

HOSPITALIZED PATIENT: Hey, Doc, you've already removed my appendix, tonsils, and adenoids. Will I ever get out of this place?
DOCTOR: Don't worry, you're getting out—bit by bit.

PATIENT: How long do I have to live?
DOCTOR: I'd say about 10.
PATIENT: Years? Days?
DOCTOR: 9...8...7...6...

PATIENT: Doctor, my husband thinks he's a python!
DOCTOR: I'll see if I can squeeze him in tomorrow.

PATIENT: Doctor, doctor, I feel like 98 cents.
DOCTOR: That's ridiculous—you're as sound as a dollar.
PATIENT: Thanks for putting in your two cents' worth.

PATIENT: I think I ate too much when I was at the beach party.
DOCTOR: Sounds like a bad case of eat-stroke.

MOTHER: Doctor, you're a quack. My kid isn't getting any better.

DOCTOR: Did you give him the medicine I prescribed?

MOTHER: Absolutely not! The bottle said "Keep out of the reach of children."

What antibiotic works well on electric guitar players?
Amp-icillin.

Why did Humpty Dumpty go to the psychiatrist?
He was cracking up.

Why did the green ogre go to the psychiatrist?
He was a nervous SHREK.

WOMAN: My husband thinks he's a turtle.

DOCTOR: Have you tried talking to him?

WOMAN: It's no use—he won't come out of his shell.

"Doctor, doctor, I feel like a kangaroo."

"Yes, you do seem a bit jumpy."

PATIENT: Doctor, my brother has lice, my sister has lice, and even my dog has lice.

DOCTOR: Hmmm, sounds like a close-NIT family.

PATIENT: Doctor, doctor, I think I'm a domino!

DOCTOR: Oh, don't be such a pushover.

PATIENT: Doctor, I think I'm invisible.

DOCTOR: Who said that?

"Doctor, doctor, I feel like an apple!"

"We must get to the core of this!"

"Doctor, doctor, I think I'm an adder!"

"Great, you can help me with my accounts!"

"Doctor, doctor, I keep painting myself gold!"

"Don't worry, it's just a gilt complex!"

"Doctor, doctor, I think I'm a yo-yo!"

"Are you stringing me along?"

DOCTOR: Nurse, how did you get the patient to sleep?
NURSE: It was easy; I told him a few of your jokes.

Vinny went to his doctor to have his leg checked.

"My leg talks to me," said Vinny to the doctor. "If you don't believe me, just listen."

Vinny's doctor put his ear to the knee and heard a tiny voice say, "I need money."

"This is very serious," said Vinny's doctor.
He put his ear to the ankle and heard the tiny voice again. "I need money right now."

"What's wrong with my leg, Doc?"

"This is more serious than I thought," replied the doctor. "Your leg is broke in two places."

What do you give a cowboy with a cold?
Cough stirrup!

PATIENT: Doctor, I swallowed a watch!
DOCTOR: No wonder you feel tick to your stomach.

PATIENT: Doctor, doctor, I think I'm a pig.
DOCTOR: How do you feel otherwise?
PATIENT: Just sow-sow.

"Doctor, doctor, I think I need glasses."
"You certainly do. This is not a hospital, it's Burger King."

"Doctor, doctor, I think I'm suffering from déjà vu!"
"Didn't I just see you yesterday?"

PATIENT: Doctor, doctor, I think I'm a moth!
DOCTOR: How did you get in here?
PATIENT: Well, I saw this light in your window. . .

PATIENT: Doctor, my wife thinks she's a grand piano.
DOCTOR: Bring her up and I'll see what I can do.
PATIENT: Are you crazy! How am I supposed to get a
  grand piano up here in that tiny elevator?

PATIENT: Doctor, doctor, I'm a burglar!
DOCTOR: Have you taken anything for it?
PATIENT: Yes, I took two VCRs and a DVD player.

PATIENT: Doctor, I think I'm suffering from poor eyesight.

DOCTOR: Hmm, let me make a note of that.

PATIENT: So you can cure me?

DOCTOR: No, so I can remember to write your bill in larger print.

What kind of specialist helps you stop sneezing? *Achoo-puncturist.*

"Doctor, doctor, I think I'm a smoke detector."

"Don't worry, there's no cause for alarm."

"Doctor, doctor, I think I'm a parachute."

"Come back tomorrow, I have no openings today."

"Doctor, doctor, I think I'm a violin."

"No wonder you're so high-strung."

DOCTOR #1: My patient swallowed his cell phone.

DOCTOR: #2: Is he all right?

DOCTOR #1: Yes, but every time he burps he gets a busy signal.

THERAPIST: I've got good news and bad news. The good news is you have a split personality.

PATIENT: What's the bad news?

THERAPIST: The bad news is I'm going to have to double-bill you.

4. JOKES 'R' US

LOU: My grandmother is on a new carrot diet.

SUE: Has she lost weight?

LOU: No, but she can see the scale much better.

What did the Christmas tree say to the tinsel?
  "Why must you always hang around me?"

What did the young blossom say to the vine?
  "Mind if I bud in?"

Who are the cleanest singers in the chorus?
  The soap-ranos.

Once upon a time there lived a prince who was cast under the spell of an evil witch. The prince could speak only one word per year. However, he could save up words so that after two years he could speak two words, and after three years he could speak three words, and so on. One day the prince met a beautiful princess and fell madly in love with her. He decided to ask the princess to marry him. Realizing he was still under the witch's curse, the prince waited and saved up a word each year for nine long years. When the fateful day arrived, the prince got down on his knees and said, "My Darling, I love you! Will you marry me?"

To which the princess replied, "I'm sorry, I wasn't paying attention. What did you say?"

Little Red Riding Hood rushed into her grandmother's house, ran upstairs, and found the three little pigs sleeping in bed. "Hey, what's the big idea?" shouted Little Red Riding Hood. "You're in the wrong fairy tale."

"Oh, you silly girl!" replied the three little pigs all snug in bed. "Don't you know this is a two-story house?"

HARRIET: I can't stand the *Wheel of Fortune*.
JULIET: Why?
HARRIET: Do I have to S-P-E-L-L it out for you?

WHERE DO THEY LIVE?

Pigs live in trailer porks.

Cows live in moo-bile homes.

Opera singers live in tenor-ments.

California birds live in condor-miniums.

Frogs live in pads.

Cats live in a-purrt-ments.

Squirrels live in nut houses.

Zombies live in doom-itories.

Homeless turtles live in shell-ters.

Cartoon dogs live in a Scooby Doo-plex.

Old Vikings live in Norse-ing homes.

Drummers live in boom-boom towns.

NUTTY NEW AIRLINES

Donut Airlines — *We fly circles around everyone else.*

DNA Airlines — *We'll never leave you stranded.*

Dental Airlines — *We're pulling out all the stops for you.*

Cannibal Airlines — *We'll fry you anywhere!*

American Scarelines — *You'll love our in-fright movies.*

Dull-ta Airlines — *You'll be asleep before we take off.*

King Oscar Airline — *We'll pack you in like sardines.*

Sunkist Airline — *Orange you glad you're flying with us?*

Fly Computer Airlines — *We hardly ever crash, ever crash, ever cr...*

Chaplain's Choice Airlines — *We'll get you there on a wing and a...prayer.*

U.S. Hare — *We're known for our short hops.*

A boy walking along the beach discovered a lamp in the sand and rubbed it. Poof! A genie appeared and said, "I can grant you one wish."

The boy thought long and hard and finally said, "I wish I had my own bicycle bridge across the ocean so I could ride my bike wherever I want."

"An ocean bridge is too difficult to build, even for someone like me," sighed the genie. "What else do you really want?"

The boy thought for a moment, then said, "At my house I can never get into the bathroom. I wish I could understand what takes my sister so long in the bathroom."

"Mmmm," said the genie, stroking his chin. "How many lanes do you want on that bicycle bridge?"

What's a worm's favorite gum?

Wiggley's Spearmint.

Did you hear about Hollywood's dumbest game show?
You win a dollar a year for a million years.

What's another name for a klutzy flower?

A whoopsy-daisy.

NEW ON DVD

Follow These Rules	by Don Dewthat
Ice Cream Your Own Way	by Howard U. Lykett
Learning Ancient History	by R.K. Ologie
Help! My Ship Is Sinking!	by Mandy Pumpes
Escape from Alcatraz	by Pickett D. Locke
Demo Derby	by Denton Fender
The Talking Alarm Clock	by R.U. Upjohn

Little Jimmy's dad was watching football instead of Jimmy. Jimmy took rocks and pebbles from the garden and plopped them into the toilet. Soon the toilet was overflowing. Jimmy's dad called the plumber. The plumber took one look and mumbled, "I see the problem, you've got rocks in your head."

What story tells the tale of a plumber who falls asleep for 20 years?
Drip Van Winkle.

What movie features classical music and Dumbo dancing?
Ele-Phantasia.

What would you get if you crossed a movie director with ground beef?

Steven Spiel-burger.

THIS IS A COMEDY!... LET'S **HAM** IT UP A BIT!!

S. SPIELBURGER
Director

SCRIPT

On what kind of bread do Japanese warriors eat their pastrami sandwiches?

On Samu-rye.

HOMER: What's small, round, and very blue?
GOMER: A cranberry holding its breath.

Why did the computer become a professional goalie?

The team needed a player who could make great saves.

What kind of Internet service does a cheerleader use?

A-O-YELL.

Why did the computer nerd take scuba diving lessons online?

He heard it was the best way to surf the Internet.

What's the difference between a computer circuit and a mom staring out the window?

One's a motherboard, the other's a bored mother.

What computers do elephants and walruses share?

Macin-tusks.

How do skunks e-mail each other very quickly?

Instink Messaging.

APOLOGIES HEARD THROUGH HISTORY

OH... SEW SORRY!

•Lizzie Borden:	AXE-CUSE ME
•Wicked Witch of the West:	HEX-CUSE ME
•The Inventor of Slime:	ICK-CUSE ME
•Rip Van Winkle:	EX-SNOOZE ME
•Humpty Dumpty:	EGGS-CUSE ME

JASON: What do flies hate most about the Internet?
MASON: The World Wide Web.

What did the computer say when the little lamb logged on?

"Ewe got mail."

Where do computer mice live?

In mouse pads.

How do pigs access the Internet?

They use America Oink-line.

What would you get if you crossed a truck with a PC?

A machine that beeps when you back up files.

HOW DO YOU KNOW WHEN YOU'VE BOUGHT A BAD COMPUTER?

• The monitor has the words *"Etch-a-sketch"* on it.

• To power it up you need some jumper cables and a chemistry set.

• Whenever you turn it on, all the dogs in your neighborhood start howling.

• The instruction manual is written in purple crayon.

• The only real chips inside are the crumbs down in the keyboard.

What's the difference between a computer programmer and a duck farmer?
One downloads, the other loads down.

What's a computer programmer's favorite opera?
Modem Butterfly.

What would you get if you crossed a glass slipper with Einstein?

Cinderella-tivity.

What would you get if you crossed boxer shorts with a chameleon?

Underwear that changes itself.

SUE: Do rollerbladers chat on the computer?
LEW: Why do you think they call them online skaters?

NIT: My dad's the best computer programmer in the world.
WIT: Why do you say that?
NIT: Because he always comes through when the chips are down.

How are computer systems like professional tennis players?

They're both good servers.

What do you call a thrifty computer on wheels?

A chip skate.

Where do mermaids put their floppy discs?

In the sea drive.

5. Class Clown

DIM: How many lazy children does it take to screw in a lightbulb?

WIT: No one knows—the kids won't get off the couch for the researchers.

How many substitute teachers does it take to change a lightbulb?

None—they just leave it dark and show a movie.

FRAN: Is it true you have an otter at your school?

DAN: Sure, all day long my teacher says I otter clean my desk, I otter pay attention...

Dweebson thought he really was the world's smartest kid. Somehow, he actually ended up on a television quiz show.

"Okay, Dweebson," said the MC. "Pick your subject."

"I'll take history for a million dollars," replied Dweebson.

"This is a two-part question," said the MC. "Are you ready?"

"Yes," bragged Dweeebson, "but I'm so smart, you can just ask me the second part."

"All right then, for a million dollars," said the MC, "the second part of the question is—In what year did it happen?"

DANA: Your chorus should sing only Christmas carols.
LANA: Why's that?
DANA: Because then we'd only have to listen to you once a year.

TEACHER: Lester, please use the word "friendship" in a sentence.
LESTER: Yesterday at the park my friend's ship sank.

TEACHER: Hank, use the word "cousin" in a sentence.
HANK: I wore a sweater cousin the winter it's cold.

When Mrs. Spencer, the third grade teacher, gave a big test to her students, Harold, the son of a millionaire, knew there was no way he could pass. Reaching into his pocket, he found a $100 bill and attached it to the test with a note saying, "A dollar per point." The next day when Harold got his test back there was a note saying, "Good try!" along with $60 in change.

TEACHER: Trudy, why did cavemen draw pictures of hippopotamuses, rhinoceroses, and pterodactyls on their walls?
TRUDY: They just weren't able to spell the names!

BUZZ: What would you get if you crossed Godzilla and a substitute teacher?
BIZZ: I don't know, but I guess you'd better pay attention in class.

TEACHER: Divide the circumference of a jack-o'-lantern by its diameter and what do you get?
LEFTY: Pumpkin pi.

KERRY: Why is Alabama the smartest state in the USA?
TERRY: Because it has four A's and one B!

KIA: The meanest kid in our school is a musician.
MIA: How do you know he's so mean?
KIA: He beats his drums and picks on his guitar.

TEACHER: Why does the Statue of Liberty stand in New York harbor?
TIM: Because the harbor is so crowded she can't sit down!

TEACHER: Why did Spanish explorers travel around the world in a galleon?
CLASS CLOWN: Because they got a lot of miles to the galleon!

Godzilla discovered her little son eating an entire football team. "What's the big idea?" said Godzilla. "I thought I told you to share everything." "Oh, all right, Mom," replied Baby Godzilla, "how about I give you a halfback?"

As a baby what was King Arthur's favorite book?
Good Knight Moon.

DAN: Why did Arthur have a Round Table?
FRAN: So no one could corner him!

LENNY: Who invented King Arthur's Round Table?
BENNY: Sir Circumference!

Two ants wandered into King Arthur's suit of armor.
They walked up one side and down the other until
they finally were able to get out safely. "Whew, that's a
relief," said one ant to the other. "Yes," said the other,
"I thought this knight would never end."

What English king invented the fireplace?
  Alfred the Grate!

What's the difference between a *Legend of Sleepy Hollow* character and a king who says, "A horse, my kingdom for a horse!"?

One's a headless horseman, the other's a horseless headman.

LENNY: I can't figure out this math problem.

TEACHER: Really? Any five-year-old should be able to solve it.

LENNY: No wonder—I'm nearly eight.

Why did the stupid goblin flunk the math test?

He couldn't find the scare root.

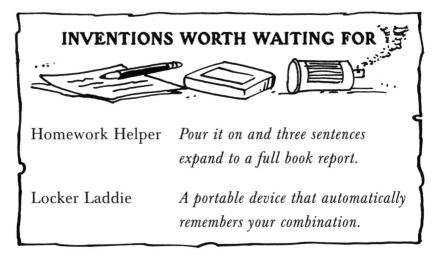

INVENTIONS WORTH WAITING FOR

Homework Helper *Pour it on and three sentences expand to a full book report.*

Locker Laddie *A portable device that automatically remembers your combination.*

CHUCKIE: The bullies at my school are so tough they eat apples.

LUCKIE: What's so tough about that?

CHUCKIE: First they chew down the tree!

Our principal is so cheap he just installed coin-operated pencil sharpeners.

TEACHER: If you act up again, I'm going to teach you a thing or two!
CLASS CLOWN: Great! I'll double what I already know.

SCIENCE TEACHER: What does your lab partner have in common with early apes?
CLASS CLOWN: Monkey breath?

STUDENT DRIVER: How did I do going around that sharp curve?
TEACHER: Ahhh...not bad, but let's stop the car and get that crumpled shopping cart off the hood.

JOE: My teacher says she's sick and tired of my appearance.
BO: What's wrong with your appearance?
JOE: I haven't made one since school started.

MIA: Did you pass the meteorology test?
TIA: Yes, it was a breeze with a few foggy patches.

Why wasn't the Tsar of Russia good to play chess with?
He was a Tsar loser.

TEACHER: Your cheating is going to lower your "A" three letter grades.
LESTER: Now that's pretty D-grading.

Why was Stuart Little sent to detention?
For being a blabber-mouse.

Why aren't elephants allowed to play ice hockey?
They can't fit inside the penalty box.

MO: What has 50 feet, lies on its back, and is very stinky and sweaty?
JO: My gym class!

What does a dentist to a hockey team specialize in?
Puck teeth.

What do ballet dancers brush their teeth with?
Tu-tuthpaste.

What would you get if you crossed an elephant with a dentist?
Someone who never forgets to brush his teeth.

DON'T SAY SLOWLY

Sam's sock shop stocks spotted sweat socks.

Kent sent Trent the rent to rent Trent's tent.

The ocean sure soaked Sean's swimming trunks.

What's yellow, has four wheels, and is full of flies?
The Magic School Buzz.

Where do one-eyed monsters look up information?
In an en-cyclops-pedia.

PRINCIPAL COMPLAINT

PRINCIPAL: Why were you acting up at orchestra practice?

CLASS CLOWN: I guess I just don't know how to conduct myself.

PRINCIPAL: What can you tell me about that outburst in art class?

CLASS CLOWN: Sorry, I'm drawing a blank.

PRINCIPAL: Isn't this your second warning not to misbehave in history class?

CLASS CLOWN: Yes, but, as you know, history repeats itself.

PRINCIPAL: Why did you run into Mrs. Leary's math class when I was chasing you?

CLASS CLOWN: I was told there's safety in numbers.

"Hurry up!" said Harold's mother as Harold dawdled on his way to school. "You'll be late!"

"What's the rush?" said Harold. "They're open until half past three."

6. A Bug's Laugh

What has a hundred feet and ninety-eight shoes?
A centipede trying on a new pair of sneakers.

What would you get if you crossed a flying insect with
a trendy homemaker?
Moth-a Stewart.

IGGY: What TV station tells the Inky Dinky Spider
   when it will rain?
ZIGGY: The Webber Channel.

What would you get if you crossed a bug with a
flower?
A forget-me-gnat.

What insect makes hit films?

Steven Spielbug.

RICH: How many cockroaches does it take to screw in a lightbulb?

MITCH: Nobody knows. As soon as the light comes on, they scatter!

What is the definition of a slug?

A snail with a housing problem!

What did the slug say as he slipped down the wall?

"Slime flies when you're having fun."

What is the difference between school lunches and a pile of slugs?

School lunches are served on plates!

What do worms leave around their baths?
The scum of the earth!

What would you get if you crossed a worm and an elephant?
Very big holes in your garden!

What is the best advice to give a worm?
Sleep late!

Why is it better to be a grasshopper than a cricket?
Because grasshoppers can play cricket, but crickets can't play grasshopper!

KYLE: What is the difference between a mosquito and a fly?
LYLE: Try putting a zipper on a mosquito!

What would you get if you crossed the Lone Ranger with an insect?
The Masked-quito!

What is a mosquito's favorite sport?
Skindiving!

How do you know that mosquitoes are religious?
They prey on you!

Why did the mosquito go to the dentist?
To improve his bite!

What's the biggest moth in the world?
A mam-moth!

What has 100 legs and goes "Ho-ho-ho!"?
A Santa-pede.

What is worse than a shark with a toothache?
A centipede with sore feet!

CLAIR: What does a queen bee do when she burps?
BLAIR: Issues a royal pardon!

FLO: What is black and yellow on the outside and
    black and yellow on the inside and drives down the
    street like mad?
JO: A school bus full of bees!

Where do bees go on vacation?
Stingapore!

7. Don't Knock It!

Knock-knock!
  Who's there?
Accordion.
  Accordion who?
Accordion to my
calculations we're lost.

Knock-knock
  Who's there?
Apollo G.
  Apollo G. who?
Apollo G. accepted.

Knock-knock!
  Who's there?
Camphor.
  Camphor who?
Camphor get my
homework again.

Knock-knock!
  Who's there?
Children's Day.
  Children's Day who?
Children's Day the
darndest things!

Knock-knock!
Who's there?
Comma.
Comma who?
Comma little closer
and give me a kiss!

Knock-knock!
Who's there?
Diploma.
Diploma who?
Diploma's here to
fix da bathtub.

Knock-knock!
Who's there?
Donut.
Donut who?
Donut make me wait
here another minute.

Knock-knock!
Who's there?
Knot.
Knot who?
Knot you again!

Knock-knock!
Who's there?
Gatorade.
Gatorade who?
Gatorade my homework.

Knock-knock!
Who's there?
Gruesome.
Gruesome who?
Gruesome since the last time
I saw you.

Knock-knock!
Who's there?
Harmony.
Harmony who?
Harmony times I gotta ring
this bell?

Knock-knock!
  Who's there?
Huron.
  Huron who?
Ouch! Huron my foot!

Knock-knock!
  Who's there?
Isaiah.
  Isaiah who?
Isaiah, old chap, care
for a spot of tea?

Knock-knock
  Who's there?
Isthmus.
  Isthmus who?
Isthmus be love.
Kiss me, you fool.

Knock-knock!
  Who's there?
Lava.
  Lava who?
Lava you to open the door.

Knock-knock!
  Who's there?
Marmoset.
  Marmoset who?
Marmoset the car keys
down and lost 'em again.

THESE JOKES REALLY **KNOCK** ME OUT!

Knock-knock!
  Who's there?
Noah.
  Noah who?
Noah bout how to
build an ark?

Knock-knock!
  Who's there?
Sparrow.
  Sparrow who?
Sparrow me the details
and tell me some jokes!

Knock-knock!
  Who's there?
Sushi.
  Sushi who?
Sushi says to me,
"Let's dance!"

Knock-knock!
  Who's there?
Thor.
  Thor who?
Thor loser, aren't you?

8. Snacks & Snickers

THE PASSWORD IS... BUGS BUNNY BUYS BAGELS!

CARROTS

ZUCHINI

SALE

Where do spies buy groceries?
At the snooper-market.

What's purple and makes you burp?
Belch's grapejuice.

What's round, hairy, and goes "Cough! Cough!"?
A coconut with a cold.

What goes well with peanut butter and says "Ho-ho-ho!"?
Jelly Ole Saint Nicholas.

A rich bratty kid was visiting a tropical island when he threw a tantrum, and the noise attracted two hungry cannibals. As the cannibals had the boy for lunch, one cannibal made a strange face to the other and said, "Hey, does this taste spoiled to you?"

What would you get if you crossed a witch with a gourmet chef?

An eight-curse meal.

What does a bully drink on hot summer days?

Cruel-Aid.

What green dip do ducks eat at parties?

Quak-amole.

What's hairy, howls, and sticks to your refrigerator?
A magnetic werewolf.

"Waiter!" snapped the angry customer as the sweat poured off his face. "It's hot in here. Turn up the air conditioner."

"Whatever you say," replied the waiter.

"Waiter!" yelled the customer a few minutes later, shivering. "It's too cold in here. Turn the air conditioner down."

"Whatever you say, sir," said the waiter.

"Say, waiter," said another customer nearby. "Why don't you ask that pest to leave?"

"Oh, he doesn't bother me," said the waiter. "We don't have an air conditioner."

GOURMET TONGUE TWISTERS

The sloppy red rhubarb made Rob's sobbing stop.

Friendly Frank flips fine flapjacks.

If Stu chews shoes should Stu choose the shoes he chews?

Lenny went to Benny's house for pizza. While waiting for the pizza man to arrive he was so hungry he ate all the peanuts that were set out in a bowl.

"The pizza won't be here for another 15 minutes," said Benny.

"I have a confession to make," said Lenny sheepishly. "I was so hungry that I ate all your snacks."

"That's okay," said Benny. "I really didn't care for them, after I sucked the chocolate off."

What would you get if you crossed the Pillsbury doughboy with a lumberjack?
Bread sticks.

One of the kids in my neighborhood is so dumb he once tried to arrange M&M's in alphabetical order.

What do you say when you see Bugs Bunny taking a bath in your mushroom soup?
"Waiter, there's a hare in my soup."

CUSTOMER: Waiter, my alphabet soup is missing a letter.
WAITER: Don't you remember—you told me to hold the P's?

CUSTOMER: Waiter, two letters in my alphabet soup are making music.
WAITER: Oh, that must be the CDs.

STU: There's a new movie out called *Planet of the Apricots.*

LOU: What's it rated?

STU: Peachy-13.

A cross-country hiker was invited to supper by some hillbillies. Stepping over two hound dogs on the porch, the hiker went into the kitchen. When he sat down to eat with the family, he noticed that the dishes were the dirtiest he had ever seen in his life.

"Excuse me, but were these dishes washed?" he asked the hillbilly mother.

"Why, they're as clean as soap and water could get them," she replied.

Scooping the food onto his plate, the hiker found himself enjoying every morsel. But when dinner was over, the hillbilly tossed the dishes onto the porch and yelled to the hounds, "Okay, Soap! Okay, Water! Come 'n' git it!"

How do short order cooks fly so cheaply?
They use their frequent fryer miles.

Do worms go to expensive restaurants?
No, only places that are dirt cheap.

Fuzzy and Wuzzy were driving through Canada when they started arguing about the proper pronunciation of the town they were in. For several miles they argued until they decided to stop for lunch. As they stood at the counter, Fuzzy asked the girl if she could settle an argument. "Would you please pronounce where we are very slowly?"

"Of course," said the girl. "This is Burrr-gerrr King."

What do health-conscious cannibals put in their stir-fry?
Toe-fu.

What do cannibals eat when they go out for breakfast?
Buttered host!

Why did the cannibals quit school?
They were fed up with their teacher.

VAMPIRE SLAYER #1: I wish our school cafeteria wouldn't serve vampire punch.
VAMPIRE SLAYER #2: What's wrong with vampire punch?
VAMPIRE SLAYER #1: It leaves a bat taste in my mouth.

How many nutty TV chefs does it take to make a pineapple upside-down cake?

Six: one to mix the batter and five to turn the oven over.

What do you get when you cross a potato with a superhero?

Spud-erman.

GILROY: Did you hear that a sneaker accidentally fell in the hamburger grinder at McDonald's?

KILROY: Wow, talk about a Keds Meal!

SCIENTIST #1: I just cloned a Rice Krispie with a cobra.

SCIENTIST #2: Sounds diabolical.

SCIENTIST #1: It is. One bite and you puff right up.

Did you hear about the mad chef who put dynamite in his refrigerator? It blew his cool!

What do basketball players like on their sandwiches?
Swish cheese.

What kind of bees makes great Chinese food?
Wok-ker bees.

What would you get if you crossed an Egyptian queen with a kids' game?
Cleo-patty Cake.

What's a ghost's favorite thing to order in a Mexican restaurant?
Re-fright beans.

What's a skunk's favorite thing to order in a Chinese restaurant?
A Peuw-Peuw Platter.

What Asian food recipe calls for both poultry and a grinch?
Chicken lo Mean.

What experimental ice cream flavor fell flat on its ear?
Cob on the cone.

9. Critter Crack-ups

What's white and black and lands on your front lawn?

A parachuting panda.

What's big, gray, and eats only carrots and celery sticks?

An elephant on a diet.

What chews tobacco, rides in pick-up trucks, and has a very shiny nose?

Rudolph the Red-Neck Reindeer.

What do you call a turtle with propellers?

A shellicopter.

What is a toad's favorite pastime?

Crosswart puzzles.

What spot would Pepe La Pew get in *Hollywood Squares*?

The scenter square.

What would you get if you crossed an elephant with a U-boat?

A submarine that eats peanuts with its periscope.

What would you get if you crossed a crystal ball with a skunk?

An animal with a sixth scent.

What would you get if you tried to cross a mouse with
Dirty looks from the mouse!

What wet London-town duck ended up on the wrong
side of the law?
Quack-the-Dripper.

Why do elephants use their trunks to eat?
So their legs are free to tap dance.

Did you hear about the boat load of lambs that
crashed into a barge carrying rams?
It was the worst sheepwreck ever.

How do sheep keep warm in winter?
Central bleating!

What do you call a ship full of rabbits?
A harecraft carrier.

What would you get if you crossed a python with an
electric eel?
A snake that's really wired.

What would you get if you crossed an elephant with a
cockroach?
*I don't know, but it's probably too big to crawl under the
refrigerator.*

What would you get if you crossed a hippo and a sled dog?

A hippopotto-mush.

What kind of cat food is popular in Tijuana?

Meow Mex.

What do you have when Moby Dick swallows a grandfather's clock?

A whale watch.

What's so bad about Octopus Airlines?

You have to wear eight seat belts.

FELICIA: Who delivers baby elephants?
DELICIA: A stork with a bad back.

What would you get if you crossed a chicken with a genie?

A rooster that grants you three wishbones.

What would you get if you crossed an electric eel with a sponge?

A shock absorber.

DANA: Are pythons stupid?
LANA: Of course, they're slithering idiots.

FRANNY: Do cows really keep up with current events?

DANNY: Sure, the other day I saw one reading a
   moospaper!

Do cows like to sing?
   Only country mooo-sic!

Where can you read about famous cows?
   In Moo's Who.

What's a cow's favorite pie?
   Lemon Moo-rang.

What goes "Ooo, oooo, oooo"?
   A cow with no lips.

Why do kangaroos love Club Med?
They hate paying out-of-pocket expenses.

SNIP: Why do elephants wear tiny green hats?
SNAP: So they can sneak into leprechaun conventions
without being noticed.

What support group do skunks join?
Odor Eaters Anonymous.

ROSE: Why are squirrels the smartest creatures in the forest?
JOSE: They only eat "A" corns.

What did the waterfowl wear to the prom?
A duckxedo.

FLO: What do you get when twenty giraffes collide?
JO: A giraffic jam.

What is the best place on a ship to watch for whales?
On the Moby Deck.

What medicine do large deer drink for headaches and
upset stomachs?
Elk-A-Seltzer.

What would you get if you crossed a peach with a pooch?
A pit bull.

What's the difference between elephants and Pop Tarts?

You need a much bigger fork to get elephants out of your toaster.

What's the difference between an elephant eating beans and the Goodyear Blimp?

The elephant has more gas.

What would you get if you crossed a llama with a hammer?

A spitting headache.

What would you get if you crossed James Bond with a large horned animal?

A spy-nocerous.

MO: A frog, a pony, a skunk, and two hunters wanted to go the fair, but a few of them couldn't afford the dollar ticket. Which ones couldn't go?

JO: Don't have the foggiest.

MO: Well, the frog had a greenback, the horse had four quarters, but the skunk had only a scent to his name and between the two hunters they only had a buck.

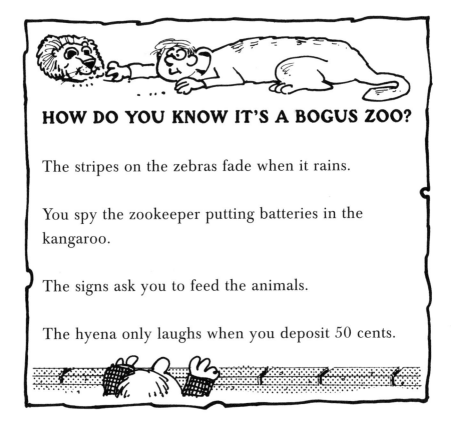

HOW DO YOU KNOW IT'S A BOGUS ZOO?

The stripes on the zebras fade when it rains.

You spy the zookeeper putting batteries in the kangaroo.

The signs ask you to feed the animals.

The hyena only laughs when you deposit 50 cents.

MOE: What do you get if you cross a grizzly bear and a harp?

JOE: A bear-faced lyre!

What do you call a little kangaroo that spends all day watching TV?

A pouch potato.

Why do koalas have pouches?

Because they can't bear to lose things.

What would you get if you crossed a cartoon dog with a doctor who talks to the animals?

Dr. Scooby Doo-Little.

What would you get if you crossed an angry dog and a lobster?

A Doberman Pinch-er.

What kind of dog wears jeans and a T-shirt and fights crime?

A plainclothes police dog!

DAN: What do you get when you cross a cute stuffed animal with a fuzzy zombie?

FRAN: A deady bear!

LLOYD: What animal do I look like when I take a bath?

FLOYD: A little bear!

FLIP: What's big, kind of cold, and plays games while on a pony?

FLOP: Prince Charles?

FLIP: Well, actually I was thinking of a polo bear!

Why was the cute little Chinese bear spoiled?
Because its mother panda'd to its every whim.

Where do pigs sleep when they go camping?
In slopping bags.

What little cottontail loved making flat bread sandwiches?
Pita Rabbit.

What Loony Tune rabbit drives kids to school?
Bus Bunny.

What smart-alecky hippo is always cursing?
A hippopotty-mouth.

What's big, brown, has four feet, and bounces?
Flippopotamus.

MACK: What would you get if you crossed a dog and a lamb?

JACK: A sheep that can round itself up!

Where do sheep buy their automobiles?
From ewes car lots.

Why did the snowman call his dog Frost?
Because Frost bites.

What would you get if you crossed a giraffe with a dog?
An animal that barks at low-flying aircraft!

What would you get if you crossed a Rottweiler and a hyena?

I don't know, but you'd better join in if it laughs!

FIRST DALMATIAN: How was your meal?
SECOND DALMATIAN: It really hit the spots.

What kind of dog comes by to keep an eye on the kids?

A baby-setter.

DAN: What has four legs, is furry, and goes "Foow, foow"?
FRAN: A dog chasing a car that's in reverse.

NIT: Why do cats chase birds?
WIT: For a lark!

What do cats read to keep up on current events?

The Evening Mews.

DILLY: I crossed a cat with a stove and guess what I got?
WILLY: A self-cleaning oven.

What would you get if you crossed a cat with a giant ice monster?

Friskie the Snowman.

What happens when you clone a little cat with a big rabbit?

An animal that coughs up huge hairballs.

Dennis and his friends were boasting about their cats.

"I taught my cat to get my slippers," said Hank.

"That's nothing. I taught my cat to get the newspaper in the morning," said Ralphie.

"You think that's so good?" bragged Dennis. "Just wait'll you see the video of my dog burying a bone."

"What does your dog have to do with it?" asked Hank.

"My cat," said Dennis, "was operating the video camera."

CLEM: What kind of cat should you take rock climbing?

LEM: A first-aid kitty!

What tiny kitten writes songs?

An itty bitty ditty kitty.

SLED DOG #1: What's up?

SLED DOG #2: Nothing mush!

11. Job Jollies

Where do great donut makers end up?
The Hole of Fame.

What store sells great clothes for trendy dogs?
Abercrombie & Fetch.

What do you do when you see an octopus with dynamite?
Notify the Bomb Squid.

The world's worst pancake cook quit to become the world's worst air traffic controller. Now he has planes stacked up all over the country.

WHEN I GROW UP

JAN: When I grow up I want to buy a bakery.
DAN: Where will you get the dough?

CINDY: When I grow up I want to be a pilot.
MINDY: Isn't that a bit over your head?

TYRONE: When I grow up I want to be a surgeon.
JEROME: You'll never make the cut.

NED: When I grow up I want to be a ballet dancer.
JED: Isn't that a bit of a stretch?

A Swedish mechanic loved working on cars so much that he spent years writing a book about his favorite automobile. At last he took it to a publisher.

The publisher thumbed through it and tossed it back.

"Sorry," he said, "we're not interested in the same old Saab stories."

What mouthwash is a must for submarine commanders?
Scope.

Did you hear about the new do-it-yourself orthodontist kit? It's called Brace-Yourself.

What is a plumber's favorite movie?
20,000 Leaks under the Sea.

Why are bakers' kids so bored?
Because they have muffin to do.

Why did the minister always videotape his sermons?
So he could watch them on instant repray.

DID YOU HEAR?

Did you hear about the moving van driver
who got carried away with his work?

Did you hear about the florist whose
future looked rosy?

Did you hear about the sheep farmer who
worked all year and had mutton to show for it?

A dweeb went to interview for a job. "What is 2 plus
2?" asked the interviewer.

"Four," replied the dweeb.

"How do you spell 'cat'?"

"C-A-T," said the dweeb.

"What is your first name?"

"Wait a minute," said the dweeb. Then he began to
sing, "Happy birthday to you, happy birthday to you..."

What entertainers get paid to pull out their hare?
Magicians.

JEFF: Do magicians do well on tests?
STEPH: Yes, they're good at trick questions.

How many mystery writers does it take to change a lightbulb?

One, but he needs to give it a good twist.

What do you call an Australian hobo who always comes back for handouts?

A bum-erang.

WITCH: Someone stole my arsenic, sulfuric acid, and bug spray.

COP: I'll send someone right over to fill out a Missing Poisons Report.

What notorious criminal gives bad haircuts?

Jack the Snipper.

Why did police think Bo Peep was involved in the big sheep robbery?

She'd been seen with a crook!

Did you hear about the robbers who stole toilets and left behind tuxedos? Now people are all dressed up with no place to go.

Who steals things off cars and gives them to the poor? *Robin Hood ornament.*

IGGY: Did you hear about the robbers who stole the truck full of whoopee cushions and the truck full of onions?
FIGGY: No, what about them?
IGGY: They didn't know whether to laugh or cry.

Where did the police put the health food crook? *Behind granola bars.*

JUDGE: Why do you always rob the same stores?
CROOK: Because the sign on the door says "Please come back soon."

What's large, gray, and peers through binoculars? *An elephant on a stakeout.*

THIEF: Give me all your money, or you're geography!
VICTIM: Don't you mean history?
THIEF: Don't change the subject.

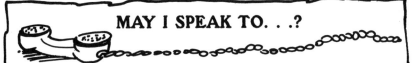

MAY I SPEAK TO. . .?

CALLER: May I speak to the boomerang champion?
SECRETARY: Sorry, can he get back to you?

CALLER: May I speak to the absent-minded professor?
SECRETARY: Sorry, he's out to lunch.

CALLER: May I speak to the famous crocodile hunter?
SECRETARY: Sorry, he's swamped right now.

CALLER: May I speak with the escape artist?
SECRETARY: Sorry, he's all tied up.

CALLER: May I speak with the undertaker?
SECRETARY: Sorry, right now he's buried under a pile
of work.

CALLER: May I speak with the head of Sanitation?
SECRETARY: Sorry, he's down in the dumps today.

CALLER: May I speak to the world's fattest man?
SECRETARY: Not right now, he has a lot on his plate.

HOW DO YOU KNOW IT'S A CHEAP AIRLINE?

• Before the flight, the passengers get together and elect a pilot.

• You cannot board the plane unless you have exact change.

• Before you take off, the flight attendant tells you to fasten your Velcro.

• The pilot asks all the passengers to chip in a little for gas.

• The navigator yells at the ground crew to chase the cows off the runway.

• The landing area is littered with passengers kissing the ground.

What did the cowboy say when he saw an elf in the cactus?

"Gnome, gnome on the range..."

Did you hear about the demolition man's son who wanted to be like his dad? He started out blowing up balloons.

What kind of motorcycle does Santa Claus ride?
Holly-Davidson.

What kind of luggage helps Santa ease down chimneys?
Soot-cases.

What kind of frozen ice cream treats do gene-splitting scientists like?
Clone-dike bars.

What's a lumberjack's favorite sci-fi show?
The Axe Files.

What would you get if you crossed a nurse with a monster?
Florence Night-n-Ghoul.

One day Iggy went for a walk and saw two men working in the park. The first man dug a hole, then the second man filled it up again with dirt. As Iggy watched, the men continued this same pattern all over the park. Finally, Iggy's curiosity got the best of him and he asked, "Why do you guys keep digging holes, then filling them back in?"

"It's real simple," said one of the workers. "There's usually a third guy who plants a tree, but he's out sick today."

A dog went into the Employment Office and stepped up to the counter. "I need a job," said the dog.

"Well," said the clerk, astonished that the dog could talk, "with your rare talent, I'm sure we can get you something at the circus."

"The circus?" said the dog. "Why would the circus need a nuclear physicist?"

Knock-knock!
Who's there?
Diesel.
Diesel who?
Diesel be the last joke in the book!

ABOUT THE AUTHORS

Matt and Philip are graduates of the School of Hard Knock-Knocks. Their other books include *It's Not My Fault Because...(Kids' Book of Excuses)*, *Totally Terrific Jokes*, *Greatest Jokes on Earth*, *Best School Jokes Ever*, *World's Silliest Jokes*, *Biggest Joke Book in the World*, and *Great Book of Zany Jokes*. They have performed at schools, libraries, and hospitals for children. Matt lives near Valley Forge, Pennsylvania, with his wife, Maggie, and daughters Rebecca, Emily, and Abigail. Philip makes his home in Austin, Texas, with Maria and their two cats, Sam and Johnnie.

ABOUT THE ILLUSTRATOR

Born in Toronto, Jeff Sinclair is an award-winning cartoonist, author, and humorous illustrator. From his home studio in Vancouver, Jeff has illustrated dozens of children's books that have been sold around the world. When he is not busy putting pen to paper, Jeff can be found playing, practicing, watching, or thinking about golf. He hopes one day to be invited to play in a PGA Celebrity Pro-Am event, preferably someplace warm. He has a beautiful swing, if he does say so himself. Jeff lives with wife Karen, son Brennan, daughter Conner, and golden lab Molly.

INDEX

95